Happy Valentine's Day to:

Color With Me!

Grandma & Me
Cupid's Valentine
Coloring Book

Mary Lou Brown
Sandy Mahony

LOVE

love is
in the
Air
HAPPY VALENTINE`S DAY

Love

Dear,

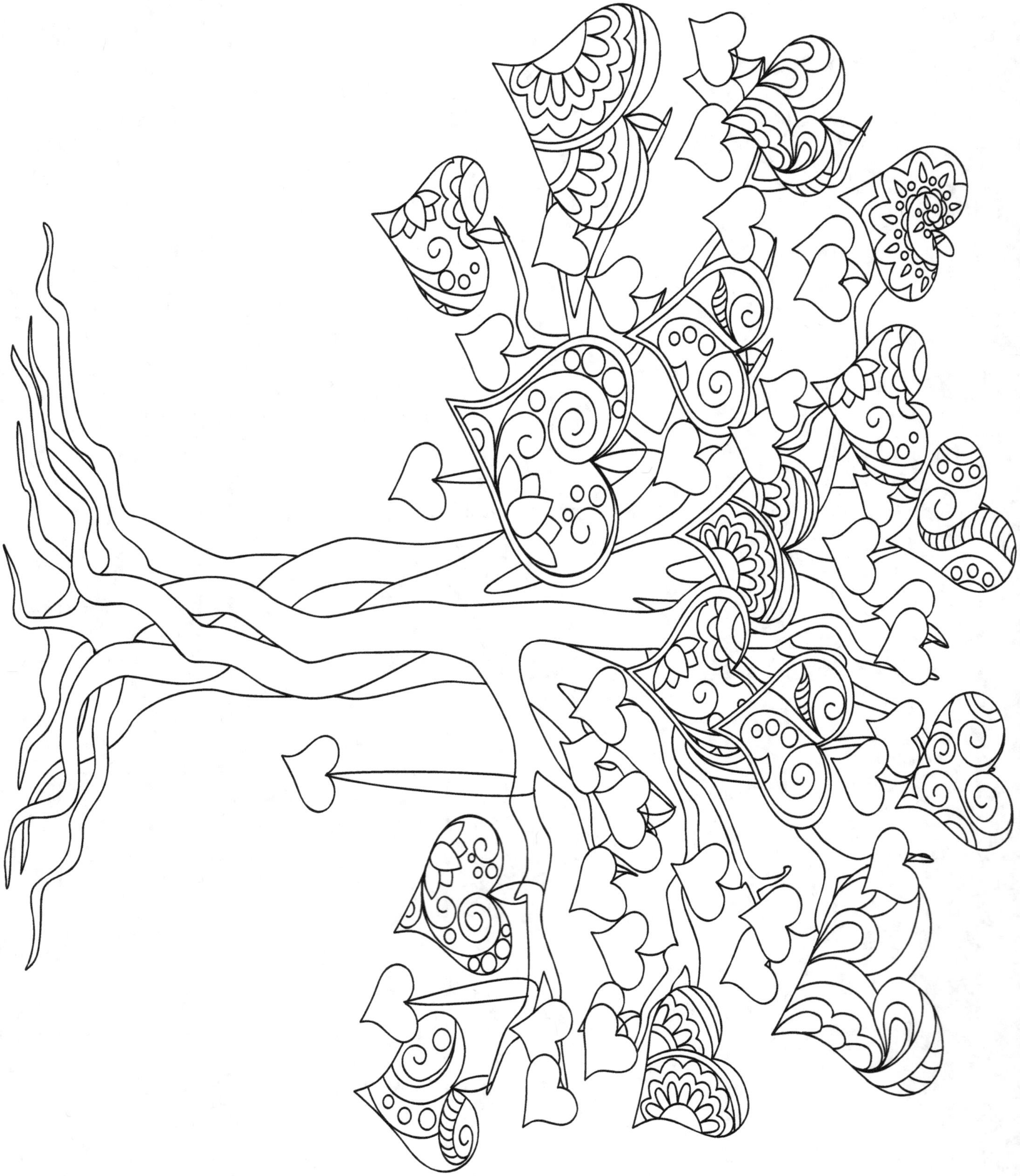

I♥U
L♥VE

HAPPY
Valentine's
DAY

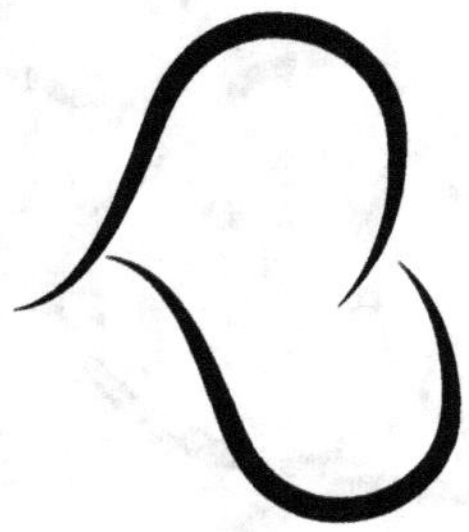

I LOVE YOU

I ♥ YOU!

I LOVE YOU!
adventurelearningpress.com

www.ingramcontent.com/pod-product-compliance
Lightning Source LLC
Chambersburg PA
CBHW081414280526
45788CB00009B/3099
* 9 7 8 1 5 4 2 4 1 8 7 5 1 *